Original title:
Succulents and Secrets

Copyright © 2025 Creative Arts Management OÜ
All rights reserved.

Author: Charles Whitfield
ISBN HARDBACK: 978-1-80581-751-2
ISBN PAPERBACK: 978-1-80581-278-4
ISBN EBOOK: 978-1-80581-751-2

Nature's Silent Keepers

In pots of green with spikes and charms,
They hold their truths, no need for alarms.
A sprinkle here, a sunbeam there,
They whisper tales without a care.

With roots that giggle beneath the ground,
They make no noise, yet secrets abound.
"Water me once," they slyly smirk,
While plotting their next funny quirk.

The Arid Mystery Unfurled

In dry terrain, they strut around,
With colors bright, they're quite profound.
What's their story? We have to guess,
In this odd game of botanical dress.

"Don't touch my leaf!" a cactus may shout,
While others giggle, they're never in doubt.
Their spines might poke, but don't be alarmed,
For in their world, you'll be charmed!

Little Secrets of Leafy Life

Under the sun, they bask and post,
In silence, they're the utmost host.
With sassy leaves and playful flair,
They dance in breeze as if they dare.

"Feed me less, or I'll throw a fit!"
In their sly language, it's a perfect hit.
A wink from jade, a nod from gold,
Their whispers of wit are quite bold.

Echoes of Drought and Growth

When rain is shy and sunbeams flirt,
These charming plants don't seem to hurt.
With laughter hidden in sturdy green,
They'll thrive and wink, oh, what a scene!

"Drought? What's that?" a succulent jests,
In their cozy pots, they're living their best.
With leaves that chuckle, they always know,
That life's a game, a funny show!

Fables of the Potted Enigma

In a pot where oddities bloom,
Lies a treasure, yet filled with gloom.
A cactus whispered to the jade,
'This isn't what the gardener made.'

The aloe laughed, a sly little cheer,
'These leaves, dear friend, are full of fear!
When the sun shines, we strike a pose,
But under questions? We all doze!'

The thyme turned sage, quite wise it seems,
'What's the point of life? Just chase our dreams!'
With each spiky tale, a giggle grows,
In this garden where everything glows.

Lock up your secrets, don't be daft,
A leaf can hide a hearty laugh.
For in each plant, a story thrives,
In pots and plots, our humor drives.

Grit and Grace in Soften Spikes

Beneath a cloak of thorny pride,
Lies tender charm, no need to hide.
With grit like sandpaper, soft as cotton,
The lessons learned, they can't be forgotten.

Prickly friends, they joke and snipe,
'You think you're tough? Just wait for ripe!'
With laughter bubbling, they dance along,
Spreading joy where spikes belong.

The soil giggles, a playful hint,
In each crack, life finds a glint.
Sassy roots wrap tight like friends,
Together, they laugh, till the day ends.

So if you topple 'neath the sun's kiss,
Just know, dear pal, it's part of bliss.
With grit and grace, we do the jig,
As soft as the puffs on a joyous fig!

The Unspoken Bond of Roots

Underneath the surface, secrets hum,
Roots giggle softly, it's all in fun.
They share old tales of blooms and woes,
While the world above doesn't even know.

A timid thorn tapped with a grin,
'I'll tell you now where the fun begins!
If you don't blush with a little poke,
Well, darling, that's just a bad joke!'

With every twist, they weave their fate,
Conspiring together—oh, it's great!'
They trade their wisdom in whispers low,
'What do humans know? Just watch us grow!'

They plot and plan beneath the sun,
Creating chaos while it's all in fun.
For with each laugh, a root can sing,
In their embrace, true joy takes wing.

Stories Held in Petal's Embrace

From blooms so bright, the tales unfold,
Of a cheeky bud, a sight to behold.
With petals wide, it jokes and sways,
'This life is grand, in colorful ways!'

A shy flower rolled into a ball,
Said, 'Blushing's tough, but I'll stand tall!'
With whispers soft, they twist and twirl,
Sharing secrets in a floral whirl.

The daisies giggled, a merry crew,
'Together, we can outshine the blue!'
As fragrances danced in a playful race,
Each petal held laughter in sweet embrace.

So when the garden's in riotous bloom,
Frolic with colors, let go of gloom.
In every flower, a chuckle waits,
In petal emojis, joy celebrates!

Layers of Green

In a pot, they sit and grin,
Winking leaves, a playful spin.
Hide and seek in soil so fine,
Count the layers, all in line.

Poking heads with cheeky flair,
While their neighbors gasp in air.
Beneath the sun, they laugh and sway,
Growing jokes in light of day.

Thorns Beneath the Surface

Beneath the smiles, sharp wit lies,
Cactus jokes, oh how they rise!
A prickly quip, a thorny tease,
Careful now, they'll catch you, please!

In the garden, boisterous pranks,
Playing tricks, they share the ranks.
Heed the thorns that hide with glee,
Or you might miss the comedy.

The Language of Petals

They whisper tales on sunny days,
In gentle shades, they dance and sway.
Petals chuckle, colors bright,
Making merry, pure delight.

With every breeze, a giggle flows,
Telling stories only they know.
A twist, a turn, they share a wink,
In floral font, they love to think.

Secrets in the Succulent Garden

Beneath the surface, giggles bloom,
Soft whispers hidden 'neath the gloom.
In the garden, mysteries tease,
Sharing tales with playful ease.

They swap their stories, sly and sly,
With every glance, a knowing sigh.
In this patch of greens and dreams,
The laughter flows in silent streams.

Hidden Roots

In the garden where whispers grow,
Cacti gossip, quite the show.
Potted plants claim they're the best,
While the weeds laugh at their jest.

Hiding treasures, like their quirks,
Aloe doing all the works.
With a prick and a sassy grin,
They plot their takeover from within.

Tiny pots with big ambitions,
In the sun, they form commissions.
Growing dreams in dusty nooks,
Trading tales like secret books.

Roots entangled, like friends are found,
Making mischief underground.
They say the soil holds all the fun,
In their world, the laughs are never done.

The Quiet Bloom

A shy flower peeks from the stone,
Whispering secrets all alone.
While daisies prance and daisies shout,
This one wonders what it's about.

Best friends with the prickly sage,
Dancing wild upon the stage.
They chuckle softly, heart to heart,
In this plant world, they play their part.

One day blooms and then they pout,
The sunlight's all they ever shout.
Yet underneath their leafy frowns,
They share ideas and silly gowns.

Roses wear their crowns so tight,
While these two giggle in the night.
A quiet laugh beneath the blooms,
Making magic in their rooms.

Beneath the Surface

Underneath where no one sees,
Worms hold meetings with the bees.
They plot and plan, oh what a scene,
In a world that's evergreen.

Tiny plants with mighty schemes,
Living big despite their dreams.
They swap their pots like trading cards,
While the ferns flirt in the yards.

A stubborn sprout trying to sneak,
Claims the sun with a cheeky peek.
With laughter bubbling underground,
They hide surprises all around.

In this realm of leafy joys,
Nature's laughter won't be coy.
Digging deep for hints and clues,
This green world never has the blues.

Eco-Mysteries

In the shade where shadows lie,
Plants disclose their alibi.
Thick with stories, thick with fun,
Photosynthesizing in the sun.

With each leaf, a secret penned,
Nature's tales around the bend.
Whispers echo in each vein,
A hundred stories hiding in plain.

The spineless ferns make a bet,
Who'll know their tales? Not just yet.
Together they create a plot,
While butterflies just sip the rot.

Eco-mysteries unfold in green,
With laughter, chaos, and serene.
In nature's arms, the truth takes flight,
A hidden world, forever bright.

The Soft Armor of Growth

In a pot quite round and stout,
Lies a plant that shouts, "Check me out!"
Its leaves, they jiggle, all so spry,
A prickly grin that winks an eye.

Water me, please! I'm feeling dry,
But not too much, or I might cry.
With sunlight stolen, it's truly bold,
In its green embrace, secrets unfold.

Tuck in a corner, snug and tight,
This little fella grows all night.
Whispers of roots dance beneath,
What a sight to behold, oh, sweet wreath!

Each day it stretches, seeking grace,
With funny quirks that light up space.
The world might frown, but here we jest,
In plant-land, laughter's truly best!

Tales from the Thicket

In a cluster tangled with flair,
A leafy gang without a care.
They huddle close to share a joke,
Rooted laughter in every poke.

"Who's the prickliest?" one plant teased,
"I believe it's him!" another wheezed.
They trade their tales of sun and shade,
In the thicket, friendships are made.

A beetle rolls by, thinking it's cool,
But the cacti chuckle, "What a fool!"
In the undergrowth, giggles envelop,
Nature's humor in every dappled shadow.

With each passing breeze, they sway and grin,
Their soft armor's on but feels like skin.
In this gathering of green delight,
The tales roll on into the night!

Heartbeats in Cactus Land

Under the sun, the cacti thump,
With a rhythm that makes the heart jump.
They sway to a beat, a quirky dance,
Who knew sharp could also prance?

A spiky fellow in a top hat,
Proclaims, "Good day!" where he's at.
With a witty wink, he tells a jest,
In cactus land, life's a raucous fest.

The heat rises, they laugh away,
Counting the clouds, come out to play.
"No watering needed, we're just fine,
A sip now takes us right on the vine!"

A parade of greens with shades galore,
They bloom in laughter, never a bore.
In heartbeats synced, they sway and sway,
In this bizarre world, let's dance today!

Tapestries of Soft Greens

A tapestry woven from shades so bright,
Each stitch a secret, hidden from sight.
In corners cozy, the greens unfold,
Tales of mischief in every fold.

Plant pals gather for a wild shout,
"Watch us grow!" is what they're about.
With leaves like hands, they wave with glee,
In a world where whimsy is key.

Sunbeams bounce on each playful face,
As they spin around in tangled grace.
"Don't be grumpy," one plant exclaimed,
"Life's too short to play unnamed!"

In each green corner, a giggle rises,
Nature's humor, full of surprises.
Beneath the skies, they tap their feet,
In a dance of joy, so light and sweet!

Hidden Lives in Succulent Spaces

In pots of green, they hold a chat,
A cactus sharing tales of that one stray cat.
With a wink and a smile, they plot and scheme,
In the land of dirt, they live their dream.

Each tiny leaf, a gossiping queen,
Whispers of mud and a broken machine.
The sun's their stage, with shadows that dance,
They gossip of llamas and happenstance.

Under the light, they throw a bash,
With soil confetti, oh what a splash!
In neighborly rows, they stand so proud,
Making the evening lively and loud.

So raise a glass to these quirky mates,
Who stir up the fun as the sun abates.
With laughter and roots, they start a spree,
In hidden lives where they'd rather be.

The Silent Song of the Mesa

On the mesa tops, where the shadows play,
The greens drop beats in their own way.
With prickly pears, they strum and hum,
A silent tune, oh here they come!

In the desert breeze, they giggle and sway,
Plant party vibes fill the sunny day.
They whisper of mischief and cactus fights,
All while bats create music in the night.

A barrel in the back throws a festive cheer,
Where whispers of plants tickle the ear.
With every bloom, a story unfolds,
Of cheeky remarks that no one holds.

So here's to the greens, with hearts so vast,
In their silent realm, friendship's a blast.
Dance on the rocks, let the laughter flow,
In the secret song where only they know.

Botanical Whispers of Resilience

In the garden's heart, they share a laugh,
Dancing through droughts on a leafy path.
With roots so strong, they stay in the game,
Old friends stuck together in nature's name.

With every thorn, they throw a jest,
Joking about the bugs that try to infest.
In the sun's bright glow, they take a stand,
Laughing loud, it's a lively band.

From tiny buds, big stories arise,
A tale of sunshine, under clear skies.
With petals like flags, they show their pride,
In botanical banter, they freely confide.

So here's to resilience, a funny twist,
In every bloom, less chance to miss.
Through wild winds and rain, they never shun,
In the world of greens, it's all in good fun!

In the Heart of the Moonstone

In moonlight's glow, they gather round,
Plants making plans on soft, cool ground.
With whispers of mischief, they play at night,
Sharing tales of stars in shimmering light.

A jade and an aloe, the best of friends,
Plotting the ways that their laughter bends.
With silvery leaves, they create a scene,
Dancing through shadows, so light and lean.

They gossip of geckos, of bugs who dare,
With every chuckle, they fill the air.
In the moonstone's glow, they spin their yarns,
Of breezy nights and adventures on lawns.

So here's to the quirks under moonlit skies,
With each secret shared, the humor flies.
In their heart, a garden, where laughter glows,
Among stones and dreams, where friendship grows.

Whispers of the Arid

In a pot, they sit so sweet,
Winking eyes, they're hard to beat.
Thirsty tales beneath the sun,
Who knew dry soil could be fun?

With tiny hats of vibrant hue,
Rumors sprout from morning dew.
They giggle in the afternoon,
Sipping gossip, over soon.

A cactus wears a cheeky grin,
Waiting for a playful win.
Napping on the window ledge,
Leaning close, they make a pledge.

Secrets whispered through the breaks,
Plenty more than what it takes.
In their stillness, joy they find,
Sharing laughter intertwined.

Hidden Thorns and Blooming Truths

A prickly friend with hidden charms,
Waves at you with spiky arms.
Don't touch here, it's not that bright,
But oh, they shine in morning light.

Under leaves, strange tales are spun,
Of daring dreams and playful fun.
Elaborate plots, oh, what a tease!
Lucky blooms to spread the ease.

A tiny voice from deep within,
Chirps like crickets, soft as skin.
"I saw you munching on that cake,"
"Don't think I won't keep that take!"

With every thorn, a laugh does grow,
The more you poke, the more they know.
In this garden, wise they reign,
Sharing joy that banishes pain.

Deserted Stories in Leafy Green

Amidst the sunburnt rocks and sand,
Lie tales hidden, never planned.
A leafy friend, all coy and sly,
With stories that would make you cry.

Once they danced under the moon,
Swapping jokes with a dandy prune.
A tumble here, a roll or two,
Now they watch the world askew.

In sway of breeze, they share advice,
"Don't be dull, live your own spice!"
With every sip of golden light,
They sprout a thought, now that's delight!

Secrets spill from stompy roots,
Oh, those tongues wrapped in green boots!
Funny fables bloom and twist,
In the garden, you can't resist.

Clarity Among the Spines

In a patch of sunshine bright,
Grows a world of pure delight.
Cacti wearing hats of glee,
Join the dance, come play with me.

Napping softly, tales they weave,
"Let's play hide and seek, believe!"
With every thorn, they poke and prod,
Funny faces, oh, my God!

What's that rustling in the shade?
An old one with a trick well-played.
"Don't mind the prick, just take a chance,"
Said the one with a spiny dance.

Mysteries bloom, oh what a plot,
In this garden, chaos is hot.
With laughter sprouted from their spines,
Blooming truths through playful lines.

Thorns and Tenderness

In a garden, spiky friends do dwell,
They wear their armor, yet they tell,
Of sweet adventures, mischief bright,
And how they laughed through the moonlight.

With a wink, they jab at passing bees,
While sipping rain through sunny leaves.
They play hide and seek with the breeze,
And tell odd jokes that would tease.

But watch your step, dear wandering feet,
These jesters guard a secret treat.
A hidden stash, with flavors bold,
Their tales of joy, forever told.

So here's a cheer for their quirky charm,
With prickly hugs, they mean no harm.
For in the wild, it's plain to see,
Funny tales sprout from greenery!

Layers of Silence Beneath the Desert Sun

Beneath the light, a shy crew lies,
With secret smiles and rolling eyes.
They hold their stories, twist and turn,
Beneath the heat, funny tales burn.

With each sunbeam, they wriggle low,
Tickling roots beneath the snow.
In quiet patches, they convene,
To plot out mischief, oh so keen!

When night falls down, they giggle bright,
Reflecting moonbeams in delight.
Each whisper shared has double meaning,
A dance of shades, always gleaning.

So if you see them, join the fun,
In silence echoing, laughter's spun.
Layers unwind in the darkened run,
And every jest blooms like the sun!

The Quiet Secrets of Fleshy Friends

In corners soft, they sit and plot,
With jiggly forms, they hide a lot.
Unfurling leaves, they smile in glee,
Guardians of joy, come see, come see!

With roots entwined, they share their laughs,
About the wind and the crazy paths.
In chubby cheeks, they stash their dreams,
Of rain-filled clouds and sparkling streams.

When sunny days befriend the night,
They whisper tales with pure delight.
Each little poke and each funny grin,
Hides a story waiting to begin.

So gather round and lend an ear,
To fleshy friends who hold you dear.
For in their quiet truth unfolds,
A heart of laughter, soft and bold!

Beneath the Surface: Untold Tales

Beneath the soil, a party brews,
With roots in rhythm, sharing news.
A wiggly dance in the dark so sly,
Beneath the earth, they laugh and lie.

From tiny twitches to secret nudges,
They celebrate life with joyful grudges.
Tales of drought and the dancing rain,
All shared in giggles, never pain.

As sun breaks through, they play it cool,
With hidden tricks, they bend the rule.
Each sprout a joker, each leaf a grin,
With stories curled where laughs begin.

So if you dig just a little deep,
You'll find their humor, like secrets keep.
Beneath the surface, in earthy trails,
Lie untold stories that tickle and sail!

Secrets Between Clusters of Shade

In pots of green, they whisper low,
A juicy tale of sun and snow.
The leaves are plump, the stories thick,
Each one a riddle, each one a trick.

Among these spines, they laugh and tease,
Plotting mischief with utmost ease.
They glance at cats, they eye the dogs,
Rustling their leaves like sneaky logs.

Some say a cactus tells a lie,
While others sip on dew from sky.
They pass the gossip in the breeze,
Over unseen cups of herbal teas.

When twilight falls, their giggles swell,
In shadows deep, they weave a spell.
So keep your secrets safe and tight,
For prickle whispers echo at night.

Echoing Hush in the Garden

In quiet plots, where greens reside,
A hush of laughter, where secrets hide.
With a twist of stem and a leaf that's curled,
They share their tales with the hidden world.

Toads croon songs, and bees unite,
A symphony of mischief in the night.
They poke their heads above the ground,
A secret society that's garden-bound.

The sun's bright rays are their master plan,
As they giggle and plot, oh what a clan!
With every droplet that falls from grace,
They whisper louder in their leafy space.

Under blooms that blush in day's soft glow,
They twirl their tales, just to show.
So if you peek where shadows blend,
Prepare for laughter 'round every bend.

The Gritty Fables of the Oasis

In sandy beds where laughter grows,
They share the tales of highs and lows.
A prickly pear, a golden sun,
The mischief here is never done.

With roots so deep, they twist and twine,
Every story sips from the brine.
'Did you hear the one about Bob's bloom?
He threw a party in the desert gloom!'

Tales of scorpions with shoes to wear,
And flamingos awkward, wild, and fair.
Each leaf a witness, each spine a laugh,
In the oasis, they've found their path.

As nights grow warm, they trade their jests,
In whispers of wind, they find their quests.
So wander near and lean on in,
For every cactus has a grin.

Tales Woven in Aloe

In a vibrant patch where the sun shines bright,
Aloe speaks softly of day and night.
With every touch of a playful breeze,
Comes laughter echoing through the leaves.

Gathered close in their spiky den,
They talk of sunburns and rogue hens.
'Last week a fairy stole my shine!'
They giggle as birds pass by in a line.

Wandering bees hum silly tunes,
While the cactus spins tales of antic moons.
'Did you see that squirrel? What a show!
With acorns flying to and fro!'

In the evening glow, their stories swell,
In every petal, there's magic to tell.
So join their circle, don't be shy,
For every tale comes with a wink and a sigh.

The Enchanted Desert Tales

In a land where cacti wear a crown,
The rumors fly as they wiggle around.
A lizard giggles, eyes full of glee,
Whispering tales of the prickly tea.

The flowers bloom with a winking flair,
While the sandy winds toss jokes in the air.
A tumbleweed rolls with a comedic spin,
Saying hello to the sun with a grin.

Under the moonlight, the shadows are sly,
They plot and they scheme while the coyotes sigh.
With spines and a smile, they share their charms,
As they wrap secrets in the night's warm arms.

In the enchanted desert, laughter is gold,
A quirky saga that never grows old.
Every twist and turn bears a punchline neat,
In this whimsical world, where mirth and mischief meet.

Layered Truths of the Lush

In the garden glows a tale so bizarre,
A pot full of green under a wishing star.
Leaves intone softly, spitting their jest,
"Truths are just layers, dress them the best!"

A curious critter hops right on cue,
Sniffing for gossip, oh what will he do?
With a wink and a twirl, he prances about,
Unraveling tales, twisty and stout.

The roots hold their secrets, tangled in fun,
Each whisper of dirt tells a story begun.
Chortles erupt from the soil so spry,
As the sun hangs above with a watching eye.

Joy blooms in patches, a laugh shared between,
Each plant a character in this lively scene.
Layered in humor, the garden's delight,
Where truths are found dancing in clear moonlight.

A Dance of Drought and Dreams

When the sun blazes down with a wink and a grin,
The thirsty rejoice for the fun to begin.
With a shimmy and shake, they sway to the beat,
Dancing in dust where the dry river meets.

A lizard scoffs lightly, sipping a sip,
In this playful ballet, there's not a dry lip.
"Let's twirl through the sand, let's leap with delight,
We'll giggle at drought under shimmering light!"

The air is alive with leaping mirth,
In dreams built of laughter, we find our worth.
While the sun sets low and the shadows creep,
These jubilant visions will never lose sleep.

In the moon's gentle glow, they frolic and spin,
Celebrating life with a cheeky grin.
Dreams woven sweetly through the arid expanse,
Invite all to join in this whimsical dance.

Intricate Vows of the Verdant

A plant in the corner swears a soft oath,
To cherish the whispers, to guard them both.
"I'll keep your tales until end of time,
In exchange for the sunlight, oh darling, sublime!"

With a nod and a rustle, another joins near,
Each promise wrapped tightly in laughter and cheer.
"Your secrets are safe, I'll not spill the beans,
Unless the wind whispers challenging scenes!"

In the grand tapestry, they weave with delight,
Witty confessions under starlit night.
Each vow trickles softly like dew on a leaf,
Growing in humor, but masked in belief.

So together they flourish, these verdant friends,
Creating a world where the fun never ends.
With intricate vows and a twist of the plant,
They giggle at troubles, a true life enchant.

Guarded Petals: Unveiling the Unseen

In a green little world, they keep their hush,
Tiny guardians, in a vibrant blush.
With spines for armor and smiles so sly,
They chuckle at raindrops as they pass by.

Each one a riddle, a story untold,
Whispers of mischief in sunlight so bold.
When no one is watching, they flaunt their charms,
Dancing with shadows, evading alarms.

The curious ones, with pots full of glee,
Wonder aloud, 'What could their secrets be?'
They giggle and wiggle in the midday light,
Feigning composure but ready to ignite.

Unseen in the soil, they plot and conspire,
Under the surface, a comical fire.
With roots intertwined in a brotherly bond,
They share little laughs, of which we're so fond.

Echoes in the Potting Soil

In cozy containers, they gather for tea,
Talking in whispers, oh look, there's a bee!
"Is it too much sunshine, or just my new shoes?"
They chuckle and giggle, sharing their views.

The mix of the dirt brings tales far and wide,
Of laughter and pranks, where secrets abide.
They swap little jokes about watering cans,
And boast of their age in succulent spans.

"Oh dear, here comes trouble! A cat on the prowl,"
They hide their allure with a giggle and growl.
With leaves pressed together, they plot their next laugh,
As sunlight pours down like a vibrant photograph.

From the corners of pots, they send out their laughs,
In a world full of wonders, precise little paths.
With each gentle rustle in the afternoon glow,
They hum little tunes that only they know.

Enigmas of the Xeric Realm

In the land of the dry, where a giggle might quake,
Tales of the droll in the heat often bake.
Tiny sentinels with humor untamed,
They play peek-a-boo; oh, they've got us all framed.

"Is it too sunny for your fave kind of hat?"
They tease each other, "Don't look, there's a cat!"
With every slight breeze, they share little winks,
In a sanctuary built on the sill where life blinks.

With roots deep in puns and leaves sprouting jokes,
Their laughter erupts like a gathering of folks.
In this arid expanse, the fun never dies,
As whispers of wisdom float up to the skies.

Secretly snickering at humans so frail,
They concoct little plots, their humorous tales.
"More water today, or light on the jokes?"
In cryptic camaraderie, the laughter provokes.

Celestial Secrets Among the Greens

In the midst of the greens, a gathering starts,
Plans for a party, with trellis and carts.
"Who's bringing the snacks? Should it be cake or pie?"
They plot through the leaves, and the giggles ensue high.

"Watch out for the spiders! They've got dance moves galore,"
Laughter erupts as they shimmer and soar.
With hues so bright, they shimmer and shine,
Twisting and twirling; oh, how they combine!

Under moonlit beams, they gather and sway,
With chatter of blooms that might come out to play.
"We'll craft a concoction of sunlight and cheer,
And sip on our laughs as the dusk draws near."

In this leafy domain, where the secrets are spun,
The shenanigans flourish, and life's always fun.
They share tiny tales while they bask and repose,
In the twinkling nightlife, where everything grows.

Shadows of the Cacti

In the desert, they whisper low,
With prickles and laughs, they steal the show.
A joke in every spiny embrace,
Who knew green could wear such a face?

Potted on windows, they plot and scheme,
Sneaky little buggers with a sunny dream.
They grin with glee, no need for a bed,
Watch out for the ones who play dead!

With water so little, they stay alive,
Mixing up shades, they know how to thrive.
Public display? Oh, what a charade!
The spiny bunch ready for a parade!

So next time you see them, give a cheer,
For every pot holds a tale to hear.
Their humor is sharp, just like their quills,
In their prickly world, there are many thrills!

Mysteries in the Succulent Shade

In the corner, they giggle and sway,
Little green jesters with tricks at play.
Behind thick skins, they hold so much fun,
Who knew they'd dance when nobody's won?

With their hidden quirks, they bloom in style,
Hiding their smiles, they tease and beguile.
Watch your step, for they might conspire,
To trip you with laughter, they never tire!

Their leaves may be plump, but they're full of charm,
Telling tall tales without any harm.
A wink from a leaf, a nod from a spout,
What's the plan here? Nobody's found out!

So when you pass by these tiny sages,
Remember their wit, with all of its stages.
In shadows they dwell, but don't you fret,
For the more you observe, the more you'll get!

Veiled Beauty in Succor

Underneath layers of vibrant skin,
Lies a treasure chest where giggles begin.
With every new growth, a tale unfolds,
These green comedians are worth their gold!

Muffled whispers in the garden's embrace,
Stories of mischief hide in each space.
Their laughter is quiet, yet sharp like a knife,
You'll find they've got a secretive life!

In pots or the ground, they play hide and seek,
Exchanging their gossip when no one peeks.
The humor is thick, like the soil they're in,
They flourish in silence, where the fun begins!

So cultivate joy with each spiky friend,
Their humor is deep, needs no pretense to send.
With every new leaf, they'll lighten your load,
In the realm of the hoarders, their laughter's the code!

The Language of Green Secrets

In every twist, there's a snicker stowed,
Laughs bubble up from their leafy abode.
Mumbling tales in a spiky tongue,
Who knew such fun could be so well sung?

Tales of the desert, the rain, the sun,
They patch up their stories with each little run.
No need for a quill, they jot in their way,
In green language, they turn night into day!

Giggling quietly when shadows grow long,
These round little rascals hum a soft song.
Every harmless poke and each scatter, they jest,
A vine-tangled chorus that never takes rest!

So next time you wander, take time to peer,
In the greenery lies a laughter so dear.
For every cactus and leaf hides a grin,
In this botanical jest, let the fun begin!

Unraveled in the Sun

In the garden, sunbeams play,
Cacti gossip through the day.
They twist and stretch with silly flair,
Underneath the bright blue air.

One green guy winks, dropping shade,
While the others are quite delayed.
Sassy plants with spiky pride,
Whisper jokes while folks reside.

A pot of laughter spills about,
As neighbors stop and twist, no doubt.
The prickly truth is hard to bare,
These leafy pals just love to share.

So grab your hat and join the fun,
In the sun where secrets run.
A leafy laugh, a sunny grin,
This plant life is where joy begins.

The Silent Oasis

In a corner where breezes play,
A silent patch keeps woes at bay.
With tongues that stick, and thorns that tease,
They hold the secrets, if you please.

A fuzzy one just rolled its eyes,
While another tries its best to rise.
Dirt whispers tales of things gone wrong,
In a desert scene, we all belong.

With every murmur, each plant's a sage,
Chilling like kings behind a cage.
A curious lick from a wandering bee,
On succulent tales, they all agree.

So curtail your worries, let them go,
In this quiet spot where laughter flows.
From cactus friends to leafy crew,
They've mastered the art of a giggle too.

Thicket of Solitude

Tangled and jumbled, they weave a tale,
In a thicket where oddities prevail.
Whispers of laughter, tucked in each leaf,
In this enclave of glee, there's no grief.

With pokes and prods, they jest and tease,
Some invite sun, while others freeze.
A riddle lies under the bark,
With answers both silly and rather stark.

There's one who rhymes, and a duo who dance,
In this patch, it's a whimsical chance.
When the sun dips low, stories unfold,
Of a merry band, both shy and bold.

So tiptoe softly in this hideaway,
Where the plants hold secrets they won't betray.
With roots intertwined and hearts so free,
In this thicket, join the jubilee!

Secrets Among the Succulents

In a nook where shades grow sly,
Cacti chuckle as they pry.
A prickly bunch, so full of glee,
Hiding jokes behind a spiny spree.

Each leaf a whisper, every branch a sigh,
Spouting tales of the clouds up high.
With a twist and a turn, they're quite the pals,
Sharing giggles in earthy halls.

On a rocky throne, the jester sits,
Trading puns while the garden flits.
With every glance, there's mischief afoot,
These tight-lipped plants are up to no good.

So don your best hat and join the jest,
In this green realm where they know best.
For laughter blooms where prickles thrive,
In this secret place, we come alive!

The Silent Sentinels

In pots they sit, so still and bright,
Guarding my snacks, from day to night.
With prickly spines and a cheeky grin,
Who knew they plotted, to sneak out and win?

One whispers jokes about the poor old fern,
While others take turns at a game of concern.
'You think you're tough?', one boasts with flair,
But they all know, it's the cat that they scare.

Green thumbs think they're full of grace,
But watch those leaves, they're plotting your place!
They laugh on sunny days, oh what a show,
As I water them carefully, they go with the flow.

So here I sit, in a leafy cafe,
With cactus pals who will never stray.
Their laughter is quiet, their humor is sly,
In this quirky patch, we all pile up high.

Whispers in the Dust

In dusty corners where shadows play,
Lies a tale of gossip that grows each day.
The tiny jade plant tells all it's seen,
While others nod, 'Oh, she's quite the queen!'

Container or pot, friendship's a blast,
As we swap our secrets from each leafy past.
'I once swayed in the breeze on a trip to the mall,'
Cackles a prickly one, who's missing a tall.

The aloe rolls eyes, 'That's quite a tale!'
'You're all soft and sweet, but I'm tough as a nail.'
They giggle and chatter, a botanical crew,
While dust bunnies spin, plotting a coup.

Roots covered in soil, they're grumpy yet spry,
Sharing wild rumors beneath the sky.
With laughter and love brewing deep in their earth,
These whispers of mine all just amplify mirth.

Echoes in the Greenhouse

In the glass house where the sunlight beams,
Grow stories and laughter, and maybe some schemes.
With leafy companions, I make quite the scene,
Chortles and giggles in shades of green.

'How tall can you grow?' the tall ones all ask,
While the short ones reply, 'Just mind your own task!'
Bantering gently, they sway with the breeze,
Trading wise cracks like it's just a tease.

The tendrils twist, sending jokes through the air,
Have you heard? That bloom just dyed its hair!
In a world full of petals and succulent cheer,
Each plant has a punchline, my dear, oh dear!

Down in the dirt, such wisdom awaits,
With everything covered in quirky traits.
There's humor in life, come take a quick peek,
In my greenhouse of giggles, where nothing's too bleak.

Touches of Drought

In a pot, they tremble slight,
Each leaf, a tale of dry delight.
Water's scarce, but smiles are found,
Nature laughs, life spins around.

Whispers float from rooted friends,
"Stay cool!" the cactus wends.
With sunburnt jokes in every spike,
They share their humor, oh so trike.

A parched tongue then crisply quips,
"Hold your water!"—sip by sips.
In dry demand, they twinkle bright,
A festival of green in the sunlight!

Oh droughty days, we love you still,
Your quirky presence, a charming thrill.
When moisture's low, we still delight,
With plants and puns, life feels just right.

The Guardian of the Garden

A prickly knight stands firm and tall,
Warding off troubles, big and small.
With leafy armor, bright and green,
He guards our greens from what's unseen.

His jagged sword gives quite a fright,
To pests and weeds, oh what a sight!
He chuckles deep, a silent cheer,
While sipping sun, never a tear.

In shadows cast, he makes his joke,
"Those weeds are just a funny cloak!"
With roots entrenched, a wise old soul,
His laughter keeps our gardens whole.

The caretaker of soil and stone,
In every thorn, his wit is shown.
So raise a glass to leafy might,
Our guardian bright, our pure delight!

Unspoken Layers

Underneath the softest fronds,
Lie tales of joy, with laughs and bonds.
Each layer hides a quip or two,
In silence speaks, with a gentle hue.

Rotund and sharp, the fun absurd,
With whispered tales, no need for words.
A succulent giggles, nestled tight,
Revealing humor, oh what a sight!

With every twist, a story blooms,
In secret spaces, laughter looms.
So much to share in every inch,
Mysteries puff, a cheerful pinch.

In harmony, these plants convene,
Their silent jokes, a vibrant scene.
With tangled thoughts, we can't resist,
A hearty laugh wrapped in a mist.

Nature's Cryptic Notes

In the soil, secrets lie in wait,
Nature scribbles on every plate.
With tiny scribes, it writes its tune,
Amongst the roots, beneath the moon.

A message here, a jest right there,
Curled leaves giggle with herbal flair.
In sunshine's glow, they grin with glee,
If you look close, you'll hear them spree.

Doodle lines in shades of green,
What's written here might be obscene!
A little pun, a cheeky pun,
Each droplet whispers, 'Life's such fun!'

So grab a spade, and join the game,
Decode the notes that show no shame.
In this garden of intrigue, we roam,
With laughter sown, we make it home.

Potted Stories Waiting to Unveil

In pots so small, they sit in light,
Whispering tales, both day and night.
With prickles sharp and colors bright,
They guard their plots, oh what a sight!

Each leaf a chat, each stem a tease,
Spilling secrets, if you please.
They giggle softly in the breeze,
Cacti dance, oh how they tease!

When the watering can starts its tune,
They sing along, a merry croon.
In clay and soil, beneath the moon,
Potted dreams do love to swoon!

So come and sit, don't be too shy,
Listen close, hear them comply.
In every corner, under the sky,
They'll spill their jokes, oh my, oh my!

Verdant Vaults of Untold Dreams

In depths of green, the laughter swells,
Jokes hidden well where nobody tells.
A thimble of water, oh the suspense,
What's next from these green, cheeky chums hence?

They plot and scheming in sunlight's glare,
Dancing gently without a care.
In pots and pans, their dreams laid bare,
They hold the punchlines of garden air.

With every glance, they wink and blink,
Never spill their thoughts, just think.
A world of fun in every ink,
From dirt and roots, they build and clink!

So tiptoe close, but don't disturb,
Their secret laughter, oh what a blurb!
In verdant vaults, they softly perturb,
Creating joy, that's their superb!

Silent Resilience in the Cradle of Earth

In sturdy beds, they quietly grin,
Weathering storms with a quaint little spin.
Their secrets buried, they bury within,
Each thorn a tale, each leaf a kin.

Through droughts and floods, they stand so bold,
Guardians of humor, tales yet untold.
With whispers quick, and laughs on hold,
They thrive in silence, their joy unfolds.

A clever cactus cracks a pun,
While aloe laughs when day is done.
In subtle shades, their fun is spun,
In every crack, a yarn begun.

So treasure these friends of the sunny earth,
For they bring joy, and cheeky mirth.
With every sprout, there's laughter's birth,
Silent jesters, for what they're worth!

Intrigue in the Arid Wild

In sandy soils, the whispers roam,
Witty banter finds a home.
In the dry sun, they puff and comb,
Secrets swirl in the desert foam.

The prickly peers share sly remarks,
While lizards dance and leave their marks.
Under starlit skies, oh how it sparks,
A stage for tales, where laughter embarks.

Each spine a story, every bloom a jest,
In arid lands, they're quite the best.
With every breeze, their charm's expressed,
Intrigue and giggles, they're truly blessed.

So venture forth, but tread with grace,
Among the green, find your place.
In wilds of laughs, the light you'll chase,
In every plant, a smiling face!

The Hidden Stories of Water Stash

Behind the rocks, a drop does hide,
A thirsty plant wears its pride.
With roots that stretch like a good old tale,
It drinks in whispers, letting none frail.

In pots so small, drama unfolds,
With sneaky sips, their thirst they hold.
They giggle softly, when no one is near,
"Just a little more, and we'll persevere!"

Who knew they could throw such a bash?
A drink-off party in every stash!
With every droplet, jokes soak the soil,
While watchful eyes keep a cautious toil.

The sun may blaze, but they won't fret,
In the desert dance, they place their bet.
Life's a hoot, in their funky way,
Secrets of hydration, come out to play.

Sips of Wisdom for the Parched

In the dry air, wisdom brews,
A leaf can teach with its morning dew.
"Take it slow and savor the sun,
Drink up quick, then have your fun!"

Cacti chuckle, oh what a sight,
In their prickly coats, they feel just right.
"Life's too short for a drought-filled day,
Get your sip, then dance away!"

When rain arrives, they put on a show,
Droplets like confetti, soaking to grow.
"Let's toast to clouds and wet feet too,
Here's a tip: stay green, stick like glue!"

So if you're parched and feeling low,
Find a leaf or two, let the good vibes flow.
In every sip, a lesson shines,
With quirky plants that share their lines.

Under the Canopy of Green

Under the shade, the giggles bloom,
In a leafy abode, there's plenty of room.
"Gather round, it's time to share,
Who watered you last? Come on, don't stare!"

The ferns whisper secrets, wrapped in light,
"Ever tried a dance with roots so tight?"
While petals flutter with winks galore,
"Join the fun, it's never a bore!"

Between the greens, the stories blend,
Of nighttime chats and roots that bend.
"Cup of sunshine, fill to the brim,
Then raise your glass for a cheeky whim!"

The canopy giggles, a riotous crew,
Plant life's a party; join if you do.
With leafy tales and smiles that gleam,
In their verdant world, nothing's as it seems!

The Palette of Desert Dreams

In the sandy stretch, colors collide,
With a wink from a flower, and the sun as guide.
"Blush like a prune, or glow like a star,
In this desert party, you'll go far!"

A paintbrush fantasy, each hue a riddle,
With pigments of laughter, just play the fiddle.
"Life's too bright for a dull old day,
Mix it up! That's the only way!"

Under the sun, the palette spins,
Golden laughter, where happiness wins.
"Come splash in colors, let none be gray,
Together we spark, let's rock this play!"

So if you wander where the cacti dream,
Know every shade holds a pulse and a beam.
The desert's whispers are not just for show,
In each colorful tale, let your spirit grow!

Tales of Sun and Shade

In the garden, a lizard grins,
Wearing shades, where sunlight spins.
Cacti gossip, a prickly crew,
Whispering tales, oh, what a view!

They lean to sun with jealous pride,
While shadows giggle, trying to hide.
A dance of light, a twirl of shade,
In this green world, decisions made!

Pods plotting mischief, daring the day,
Beans argue sprout and twirl in play.
With petals sassy, they take the lead,
Who knew plants had such a funny creed?

In laughter, they share a cheeky jest,
A tale of growth, a little test.
With every bloom, a prank unfolds,
In the patch where sunlight scolds!

Between Thorn and Touch

There's a cactus with a chip on its green,
Claiming its prickle is a grand routine.
Each time I reach, it sent me flying,
With a laugh so loud, you'd think it's lying!

A succulent's winking, it's painted bright,
It sways with pride, ooh, what a sight!
Sipping the sun, it splashes with glee,
While nearby thorns plot a sticky decree.

A dance of petals, a tussle of fun,
Between sharp edges, oh what a run!
The drama unfolds, a playful affair,
With laughter and green hearts unaware.

But beware the sharp fruit, oh so sly,
It's a jester cloaked in a prickly tie.
We giggle together, those who dare touch,
Knowing the secrets may hurt too much!

Solace Among the Succulent Spines

In a pot of joy, a quirky plant,
Joking around, oh how it can chant!
It whispers softly, humor entwined,
A refuge found among leaves so kind.

The blooms trade stories, a coronation,
With petals that sparkle in wild elation.
Prickles are just a playful disguise,
For soft little secrets in each blossom's eyes.

The sagebrush nods, quite wise and grand,
As puns fly around in this green wonderland.
A sprout grins wide, with colors that clash,
When it bursts into giggles, all thorns turn to ash.

In their cozy circle, no need to pretend,
With each prick and poke, it's laughter we send.
Join this ballet of green, don't shy,
In the joy of the garden, we happily fly!

Sentinel Blooms: Guardians of the Desert

Amidst the sands, a guard stands tall,
An awkward bloom with a glorious sprawl.
Waving its arms, it shouts, "Stay here!"
While prickle-laden friends cheer, "Oh dear!"

The watchful watchman, blooms like a star,
Cracking up cacti, they laugh from afar.
With spines as armor against the dull night,
It twirls with glee, a comical sight.

In the moonlight, they share bad jokes,
Singing out loud, these peculiar folks.
With each hearty laugh, sand dunes sway,
In this hilarious wood of green ballet!

So as the sun sets on this comical show,
Remember the blooms and their silly glow.
Guardians they may be in desert's forlorn,
But they're masters of fun and floral adorn!

Without a Word, They Speak

In pots of green, they sit so sly,
Whispering truths that make us sigh.
With a wink and a twist, they show their flair,
No need for gossip, they just don't care.

With spines like secrets, they guard their tales,
Each leaf a witness to our trails.
In silence, they chuckle, just like a cat,
As we fuss and fret over this and that.

When thirsty, they dance, a jig in the sun,
Grinning widely, they've already won.
They thrive on neglect, just watch them smirk,
While we're all panicked, they simply lurk.

So next time you see them, give a grin,
For they know our lives and the chaos within.
In their quiet way, they rule the scene,
Masters of mischief, oh so serene.

The Lush Chronicles of Survival

In the wild of pots, they learn to thrive,
Beneath our reign, they just seem alive.
While we can grumble about this and that,
They chuckle in green, 'Look at that!'

They drink from the sun with a cheeky glance,
While we're worried, they twist and prance.
"Too much water? Ha! We'll just wait,"
They giggle in silence, it's never too late.

In a world of chaos, they plot and scheme,
Dancing in dirt like a sweet little dream.
They'll outlive us all, just watch them twirl,
While we chase around in a mad world swirl.

So here's to our friends, the leafy brigade,
With their green thumbs-up, they've got it made.
In the tales of the wild, they play their part,
With spines full of wisdom and a joyful heart.

Gardens with a Gossamer Veil

In the garden realm, they play hide and seek,
With laughter so light, and wisdom unique.
Wrapped in their robes of velvety green,
They plot their schemes and dream what's unseen.

With every sunset, they share a toast,
Joking of drought, "We're the ones that boast!"
They peek through petals, giggling in mirth,
Who knew the ground held such playful girth?

In each little crevice, a chuckle's concealed,
As earthbound jesters, their humor revealed.
While we fret with worries, they just shake their heads,
"Why not just lounge in our leafy beds?"

So tiptoe through blooms, be gentle and wise,
For under their charm lies a world in disguise.
With secrets aplenty, they dance in a line,
Whispering chuckles that are truly divine.

In the Spine's Embrace

In corners so cozy, they crown the room,
With a prick and a laugh, they chase away gloom.
Wrapped in sharp armor, they play the game,
"Approach with care, we're wild and untame!"

They gather in groups for a gossiping spree,
With blushing green cheeks, oh can't you see?
"Did you hear what the cactus told the jade?
They say there's too much light—we might just fade!"

While we bumble around, they sit so still,
With twinkles of mischief, they've got the thrill.
"Water twice a week? We'll show you our way,
Just leave us to bask in our sunny ballet!"

So let's raise a toast, to the guardians quiet,
In their spine-wrapped embrace, they start a riot.
With each secret shared, a laugh blooms anew,
In gardens of humor, with joy in their view.

Beneath the Surface of Arid Whispers

In a pot where green things hide,
Lies a tale of roots with pride.
Each leaf a cover, a subtle grin,
Whispering secrets of where they've been.

One sprout claims it's quite the star,
While another just dreams of a jar.
They debate if rain is a myth,
Or just a rumor of late-night tithes.

In a world of sun and quirky cheer,
They rehearse their stories, with nary a fear.
Each twist and curl a plot device,
Joking about mud, oh so very nice!

So when you glance at life so quaint,
Remember these tales, they're never faint.
For beneath the surface, oh what fun!
Laughter in green, and the summer sun.

The Leafy Conundrum of Growth

In the corner sits a strange affair,
A cactus pondering its existence bare.
With spines for style, it strikes a pose,
Sipping sunlight with mysterious prose.

A fern nearby flips its leafy mane,
Claiming wisdom in every grain.
Yet every day it's lost in thought,
About how many waters it has sought.

The succulent crowd is quite a trip,
With rumors of blooms and the odd little slip.
"They say I need love," one succumbs,
But it's really just water that cuts the crumbs.

So gather 'round in your sunny patch,
Where gossip flows without a catch.
For in this green world, laughter's the key,
To unlock the joke of being free!

What Lies Beneath: Tales of Resilience

Beneath the soil, tales unfold,
Of daring deeds and ambitions bold.
A rogue little root, with a mischievous cheer,
Wonders if it's time for a leap in the sphere.

One thistle says, 'I'm tough as nails!'
While a bloom blushes and tells long tales.
They swap their stories, both wild and free,
Of storms they've braved and how they flee.

With every push through the hardened crust,
They're scribbling chapters in the earth's rust.
A giggle rises with each sprouting's fight,
As they embrace the darkness, seeking the light.

So next time you ponder the green parade,
Remember the joys that nature's made.
For in each little sprout, a story runs deep,
With laughter and secrets, in silence they keep.

Sheltered in Green: Nature's Quiet Rebellion

In a pot filled with whimsy and cheer,
A leafy revolt whispers in your ear.
With each sly curl, there's mischief at play,
As they mock the droughts that come their way.

A plucky plant claims it knows the trick,
While others debate if they'll bloom or flick.
They chuckle at storms that may come their way,
Sipping sunshine on a bright, leafy day.

The garden's alive with a humorous stance,
Each prickly guardian ready to prance.
So when they sway in the softest breeze,
They laugh at the world with effortless ease.

Join this riot of green, grab a seat,
For here in their realm, life's truly a treat.
In the shadows of pots, laughter thrives true,
As nature's rebellion plays peek-a-boo!

Dreaming Among Cacti Shadows

In a garden where the prickle plays,
Little green friends dance in the rays.
Whispers of mischief in the sun's embrace,
They plot and they scheme, a playful race.

One ballsy bloom claims it's the best,
But all of them know who's truly blessed.
With tiny arms raised, the ruckus begins,
In this prickly realm, laughter always wins.

In moonlight, the shadows begin to prance,
Cacti giggle as they join the dance.
A rendezvous where the oddball thrives,
In their spiny world, hilarity survives.

Though still and quiet, they never lack cheer,
With poky jokes shared between each sphere.
As night dims down, their antics subside,
Dreams of green tomfoolery bouncy inside.

The Serene Covenant of the Earth

In a land where the dry air sings,
Mighty plants wear their quirky bling.
With dashes of green and hues so spry,
They chuckle at those who say they're shy.

A burly fellow takes on the sun,
Laughs at the clouds, says, "What's the fun?"
With arms outstretched to the endless blue,
He whispers tales like the wind to woo.

Nestled among rocks, a sly little crew,
Chatting about the sun and dew.
Their secrets bubble like a fountain fresh,
Bursting with laughter, it's quite the mess.

But each day ends in a solemn pact,
That the sun will rise and no one will act,
Too serious, oh, they'll keep it light,
In their vibrant kingdom, all feels right.

Quiescence in the Dry Lands

Beneath the surface where shadows creep,
Thieves in the night plan and peep.
A thistle snores, dreaming of cake,
While the others conspire, for mischief's sake.

An eager sprout thinks it's sly and slick,
Let's swap our pots for a funny kick.
But roots get tangled in chaos unplanned,
Such antics are not what the gardener planned.

With laughter bouncing from prickly spines,
A riot of green, where humor shines.
They sparkle in sunlight, no frown in sight,
For in this dry land, they'll do what feels right.

When the dusk settles, stories unfold,
In belly laughs, the plants take hold.
This land may be dry, but they don't despair,
For humor's the nectar that flows through the air.

The Spiky Narratives of Survival

In the wilderness, tales twist and turn,
With each prickly plot, lessons to learn.
A stubborn sagebrush brags with glee,
"I sell good humor—come buy some from me!"

Each bold little sprout, a character grand,
Delivers a punchline with just a hand.
Over rocks and sand, they spread the fun,
In their hilarious world, there's always a pun.

To the rhythm of wind, they shake and sway,
Making jokes about the sun's harsh play.
"Who needs water when we've got style?"
These spiky treasures wear laughter like a guile.

As dusk lingers on, the mischief takes flight,
Stars in the sky share secrets at night.
For in every thorn, there's a story's embrace,
In this spiky realm, humor finds its place.

Silent Gardens of the Unknown

In a pot, a plant draws a grin,
Hiding truths where it's been,
A cactus wearing a smile pout,
Whispers of joy when there's doubt.

In shadows, where they conspire,
Laughter blooms, never tires,
With each leaf, a chuckle or two,
Who knew green could be so askew?

When watered with gossip, they thrive,
Rumors in soil keep them alive,
They plot under the sun's watchful gaze,
In their world, a wild, green maze.

And yet, they keep their tales entwined,
Roots entangled, secrets defined,
But hey, with humor, they survive,
In their world, we're all alive!

Resilient Roots and Quiet Echoes

Beneath the soil, a party swells,
Rooted friends sharing silly spells,
"I'll outgrow you," one cheekily said,
"Better with me than cold, hard bread!"

Echoes of laughter rise from the dirt,
Tickling the leaves, dressed in their shirt,
"Are we plants? Or just fancy fools?"
Underneath, they draw up the jewels.

Each leaf tells a joke, unaware,
In the stillness, none have a care,
Grow tall, grow wide, they take a stance,
In this garden, they all dance.

In harmony, they flourish, wear proud,
Singing their tunes, cheeky, and loud,
With roots intertwined, like friends who care,
Their echoes of laughter fill the air!

Succor in the Silhouette

Silhouettes of charm in the dusk,
Each corner hides secrets, a playful husk,
A moonlit glow, where whispers roam,
In every shadow, a plant calls home.

Cacti with spines, pointy and bold,
Joking about the tales they've told,
"Sit down, don't prick your heart here!"
In this garden, all laughs and cheer.

With leaves that dance to the nighttime breeze,
Each one tickles with laughter and tease,
"Shh, don't spill the beans," they insist,
But every petal joins in the twist.

Under the stars, their stories collide,
In the hush, their playful pride,
With clandestine meetings in the night,
These leafy jesters keep the light!

Deceptive Blooms in Drought

In drought, they wear a vibrant mask,
Scheming away, if you dare to ask,
"Are we thirsty, or merely sly?"
Every blossom whispers a lie.

Petals bright, but roots unsure,
Underneath lies a life obscure,
"Fill my cup," they jovially plead,
While sipping secrets, planting the seed.

In arid lands, they trick the eye,
With colors bold, they dance nearby,
"Need a drink? Just hang on tight,"
They laugh in shadows, out of sight.

With twinkles and winks, they survive,
In a world where only the clever thrive,
"They think they know, but how wrong they are,"
In this garden of jests, they shine like a star!

Nature's Hidden Codex

In pots of green, a mystery lies,
A cactus sneers with spiky ties.
It holds the tales of sun and shade,
In tiny worlds, where jokes are made.

From leaves so plump and round, they grin,
A giggle grows as they begin.
A succulent said, 'I can't keep still!'
'The more you water, the less I thrill!'

With every drop, they play a game,
A thirst for fun, yet not for fame.
They hide their laughs in dusty seams,
Unraveling nature's silliest schemes.

So next you pass by those leafy traits,
Remember their jests, their funny fates.
For in their roots, a chuckle's steeped,
In Nature's code, our laughter's kept.

Whispers of the Arid

In a desert patch, where dry winds gleam,
A sagebrush chuckles, plotting a scheme.
It whispers tales of sunburned joy,
While cheeky agaves play with coy.

A lizard scoffs as he passes by,
'You think you're tough? Just watch me fly!'
As prickly pears flash their fruity smiles,
They gossip sweetly of distant miles.

Around the cacti, the shadows dance,
With mischief brewing at every chance.
Each spine a secret, each bloom a hoot,
They make the sun blush with their cute loot.

So tiptoe softly, hear their delight,
For in the dry air, laughter takes flight.
With every breeze that stirs the sand,
A joke unfolds in this arid land.

Green Enigmas

In the garden's heart, a wonder unfolds,
With emerald whispers and stories bold.
The jade plant cackles, 'Watch my glow!'
'This green disguise? Oh, what a show!'

A barrel cactus rolls its eyes wide,
'Why stand in line when you can slide?'
As agave grins beneath its crest,
It claims to know the ultimate quest.

The air is thick with peculiar charms,
Where every petal spreads out its arms.
Each leaf conceals a playful wink,
Giggling softly, they plot and think.

So pull up a chair, sit down for a spree,
Let nature's fun reveal its key.
For in the garden, humor reigns,
With every thorn, a laughter gains.

Hidden Thorns

In a patch where laughter's slyly sown,
Thorns hide treasures that sparkle and moan.
'Careful!' warns one with a cheeky grin,
'You poke too close, that's where I win!'

With every jab, a joke's unleashed,
A rose pretends it's not a beast.
And yet the laughter fills the air,
As blooms crack jokes while spines declare.

"Oh dear friend, you thought I'd weep?
Just you wait, my secrets run deep!"
Behind each prick lies a punchline sweet,
Nature's humor is quite the treat.

So tread with jest and dance around,
For hidden thorns wear laughter's crown.
In every garden lies a tale,
Where humor blossoms, never stale.

Desert Blooms and Hidden Rooms

In the dry of the day, things pop up with glee,
A prickly little party, just for me!
Tiny pots whisper tales, oh so sly,
Of secrets tucked away, beneath the sky.

Cactus in slippers, they dance with flair,
While the thirsty ground chuckles, 'There's plenty to share!'
Dancing shadows slip in, making a fuss,
While garden gnomes grin, 'We're here for the bus!'

Each bloom has a story, a twist and a turn,
Of watering cans and sunburns that burn.
With each sunny laugh, I water the tale,
In this garden of wonders, we'll never fail.

So gather your friends, both leafy and green,
For the wildest of nights, it's quite the scene!
With cocktails of nectar, we'll drink 'til we swoon,
In the land of surprise, where flowers are tunes.

The Cactus Memoir

Once there was a prickly with dreams so immense,
He sought to be smooth, it just didn't make sense.
In an awkward embrace, he slipped on some cream,
But the results were absurd, like a bad fruit-themed dream.

With a hat made of soil and sunglasses too,
He strutted around like he was brand new.
His friends all just laughed, with vibes oh-so-true,
'Cacti can't tan, we're all misshapen too!'

One day a squirrel came, with questions galore,
'Do you really feel spiky, or beg to explore?'
"Dear fuzzy little friend, I just want a hug,
But I fear that my spikes make me look like a thug!"

So they plotted and planned a soft family tie,
Where thorns would be cushions, and none had to cry.
With laughter like thunder, they turned up the heat,
In a memoir of joy, with friendships so sweet.

Leaves of Mystery

In a pot on the shelf, a leafy chap sat,
He'd twirl and he'd swirl, and wear quite the hat!
With secrets entwined in his luscious green fronds,
He giggled at whispers like a game of absconds.

His neighbor, a rogue with spikes to the max,
Claimed he could tell tales about moonlit snacks.
'A feast of the dust bunnies, held by the night,
With a side of moonbeams, oh what a delight!'

But the rumors spread wild, like weeds in a maze,
Every leaf seemed to plot in a giggling haze.
'We're the masters of jest, we shall not reveal,
Our recipes bold, don't worry, no meal!'

So under the stars, their giggles grew loud,
In leafy confessions, they all felt so proud.
With laughter and leaves, they fluffed up the night,
Creating a garden where fun took the flight.

Soft Shadows in Sandy Soil

In sandy plots where the giggles roam free,
A succulent sage shared tea with a bee.
'Do you know the best secret of this sunny spot?'
'Napping under the sun is truly a plot!'

Shadows danced lightly, like whispers of fun,
As ferns told tall tales, soaking up sun.
They spoke of a code, held by the moon,
When shrubs sway together, it's the best kind of tune.

With spouts of green, they played hide and seek,
In a landscape of joy, where laughter's unique.
A tumbleweed joked, 'I'm just passing through!'
While all gathered 'round, become part of the crew.

So next time you wander, to the land where they thrive,
Remember the giggles that keep them alive.
For beneath every leaf, there's a cheeky delight,
In the soft sandy shadows, they party all night!

www.ingramcontent.com/pod-product-compliance
Lightning Source LLC
Chambersburg PA
CBHW072216070526
44585CB00015B/1358